Colorado Activity Book

by Paula Ellis, illustrations by Anna Kaiser

This book is dedicated to my cousins Jim and Shari Fraker, who have a deep love and passion for Colorado, her land, her people and her wild places.

—*Paula*

Cover design by Jonathan Norberg
Book design by Lora Westberg

10 9 8 7 6 5 4

Copyright 2010 by Paula Ellis
Published by Adventure Publications
An imprint of AdventureKEEN
820 Cleveland Street South
Cambridge, Minnesota 55008
(800) 678-7006
www.adventurepublications.net
Printed in China

ISBN: 978-1-59193-241-3

Welcome to Colorado

The meaning of Colorado is "red colored," from the Spanish word that probably refers to the once-red Colorado River, or the red rock of the Colorado Plateau, where Spaniards first entered the region.

Colorado has three kinds of landform regions from east to west—plains, mountains and plateau. Each region is unique and covers the U.S. far outside Colorado borders.

The Great Plains is a great prairie grassland that covers portions of 10 states from Canada to Texas. This giant flatland slopes and drains rivers toward the east. Most cities in Colorado are on the Great Plains, just east of the Rocky Mountains' Front Range because the weather is nice here.

The Rocky Mountain Range is the longest and highest in the lower 48 states. It covers 2,980 miles, from Canada to New Mexico. Peaks are from 7,500 to over 14,000 feet tall—at the highest altitudes, climate conditions are similar to the Arctic Circle (brrrr!). At 14,433 feet, Mt. Elbert is the highest peak in the range. There are 53 mountains in Colorado over 14,000 feet high, including Pikes Peak and Longs Peak.

The Colorado Plateau is a high flatland in western Colorado. It covers parts of three other states—Utah, New Mexico and Arizona, where it ends at the Grand Canyon. The Colorado Plateau has the highest concentration of national parks in the country! Sometimes called Red Rock Country, it is famous for its dramatic, semi-desert landscapes. The Colorado River drains the Colorado Plateau through the Grand Canyon.

In Colorado, I want to go:

☐ rafting	☐ sightseeing	☐ hiking	☐ skiing/snowboarding
☐ hiking	☐ biking	☐ climbing	☐ wildlife watching
☐ shopping	☐ sledding	☐ fishing	☐ horseback riding

In Colorado, I want to visit:

☐ a mine	☐ Pikes Peak	☐ The Four Corners	☐ Denver Zoo
☐ Quartz	☐ a river	☐ Dinosaur Ridge	☐ Great Sand Dunes
☐ Grand Mesa	☐ Denver	☐ Garden of the Gods	☐ a ranch

What do you like best about Colorado?

Colorado Map

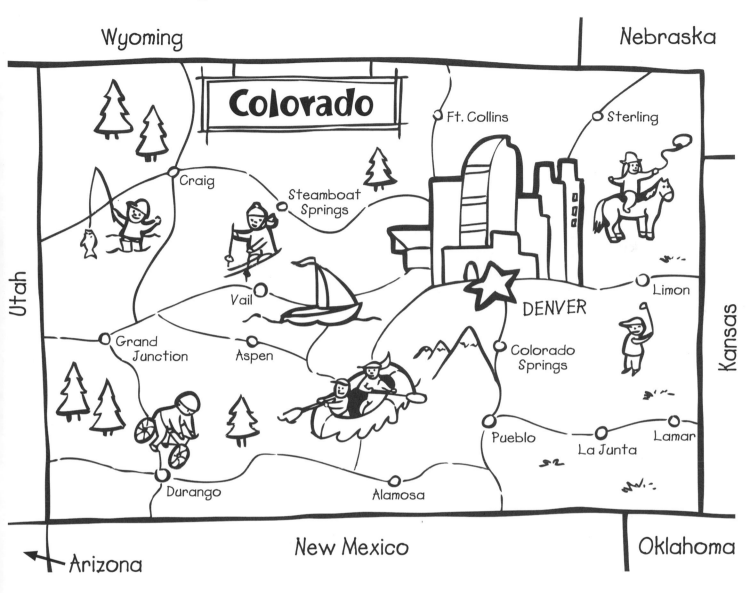

Wyoming　　　　　　　　　　　　　　Nebraska

Colorado

Ft. Collins　　　　Sterling

Craig

Steamboat Springs

Vail

DENVER

Limon

Grand Junction　　Aspen

Colorado Springs

Durango　　　　Alamosa

Pueblo　　La Junta　　Lamar

Utah

Kansas

Arizona　　　　New Mexico　　　　Oklahoma

Use the map to find the answers.

The 8th largest state in the United States, Colorado is shaped like a:

☐ piece of pizza　　　☐ rectangle　　　☐ circle　　　☐ snail

How many states share a border with Colorado?

☐ 12　　　☐ 7　　　☐ 8　　　☐ What, me count?

Circle the names of the states that border Colorado:

Wyoming	Minnesota	Nebraska	Kansas	New Jersey	California
Mississippi	Arizona	Pennsylvania	Mars	North Dakota	Oklahoma
New Mexico	England	Missouri	Hawaii	Utah	Florida

Colorado State Symbols

State Flag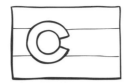

State Animal Rocky Mountain Bighorn Sheep

State Bird Lark Bunting

State Fish Greenback Cutthroat Trout

State Reptile Western Painted Turtle

State Tree Colorado Blue Spruce

State Flower Colorado Blue Columbine

State Insect Colorado Hairstreak

State Fossil Stegosaurus

Colorado Fun Facts

On August 1, 1876, Colorado was the 38th state admitted to the United States.

World's largest flat top mountain: Grand Mesa.

Highest road in North America: Mt. Evans Scenic Byway, which dead ends 14,258 feet above sea level, at Mt. Evans' summit.

Highest continuous road in North America: Trail Ridge Road (US 34) through Rocky Mountain National Park. Highest point: 12,183 feet.

Longest continuous street in the US: Colfax Avenue, Denver.

One mile high, exactly: The 13th step of the state capitol building, Denver.

World's largest stock show: The annual National Western Stock Show & Rodeo, held in Denver, has the most animals and is one of the world's largest indoor rodeos.

World's highest cog train: It takes passengers to the top of Pikes Peak at 14,110 feet. Train cars have a central gear, a cog wheel, that meshes to a special track— it helps the train make steep climbs.

Melon capitol of the world: It's what the town of Rocky Ford calls itself for their extra-sweet cantaloupe and watermelon. They also grow crops just for seeds—vegetables, herbs, flowers, and of course—melons!

Highest suspension bridge in the world: Royal Gorge Bridge—1,053 feet high.

Only place where four US states meet: The Four Corners Monument, where Colorado, Arizona, New Mexico and Utah meet in the southwest.

Home of the astronauts: Sixteen NASA astronauts come from the University of Colorado in Boulder, including Scott Carpenter, John Swigert, Stuart Roosa and Vance Brand. Plus, astronaut Gerald Carr is from Denver.

State record temperatures:
- 118 degrees on July 11, 1888.
- -61 degrees on February 1, 1985.

US National Historic Landmarks:
- Kit Carson County Carousel, Burlington, 1905—the only antique carousel with all of its original paint—and it still works, so you can ride it!
- Lowry Ruin, 1060—Ancient Pueblo Peoples (American Indian) archaeological site, excavated in the 1930s.

A-B-Cs of Colorado

Take a trip through the alphabet in the State of Colorado

A is for **Air** Force Academy in Colorado Springs

B is for **Bighorn** Sheep that live in the Rocky Mountains

C is for **Cowboys** who ride the Colorado Prairie

D is for **Dinosaurs** that once roamed the land we call Colorado

E is for **Elk** that make their home in the mountains

F is for **Four** Corners, where Colorado meets Utah, Arizona, New Mexico

G is for **Gold** found in the ground and streams of Colorado

H is for **Horses** that work on the ranches in Colorado

I is for **Indians** who have a long history in the land of Colorado

J is for **Jolly** Ranchers; they were created in Golden, Colorado

K is for **Kit** Carson, a trapper and guide who explored Colorado

L is for **Longhorn** cattle who graze in the eastern plains

M is for **Mountains**; Mt. Elbert is the highest peak in Colorado

N is for **Navajo**, the largest Native American tribe in the United States

O is for **Olympic** Center where United States athletes train

P is for **Pikes** Peak, the most visited mountain peak in the U.S.

Q is for **Quartz**, Colorado, one of many ghost towns in the state

R is for **Rodeo**, a favorite sport of cowboys in Colorado's history

S is for **Ski**, a popular sport in the mountains of Colorado

T is for **Tunnel**; the most famous is the Eisenhower-Johnson

U is for **Underground** where you can find gold, silver and diamonds

V is for **Vinegar** Hill, a favorite sledding hill in Ouray, Colorado

W is for **Wheat**, the major food grain grown in Colorado

X is for **X-treme**; mountains make good places for extreme sports

Y is for **Yucca**, a plant that Native Americans used to make soap

Z is for **Zebulon** Pike, an explorer; Pikes Peak was named for him

Zebulon Pike

Zebulon Montgomery Pike Jr. was a soldier and an explorer. On one trip, now called the Pike Expedition, he mapped the High Plains from Missouri to Colorado. Although he never reached the top of Pikes Peak, it is named for him. His trip is often compared to Lewis and Clark's famous voyage to the Pacific Ocean.

Zebulon Pike's daughter, Clarissa, married John Harrison, son of President William H. Harrison.

Rocky Mountains

The Rocky Mountain range runs through western Colorado from British Columbia in Canada to New Mexico. Mount Elbert is 14,433 feet high, making it the highest peak in Colorado as well as the highest in the Rockies. More than 50 peaks in Colorado are known as "fourteeners," because they are 14,000 feet or higher.

 The eastern side of the Colorado Rockies is called the Front Range and the western side, the Western Slope.

Winter Fun

Some parts of Colorado get over 100 inches of snow each year. All this snow makes it a popular place to go skiing or snowboarding. Vail Mountain, at 12,250 feet, is home to Vail Ski Resort, the largest ski area on one mountain in North America. Other favorite winter sports areas include Aspen, Breckenridge and Steamboat Springs.

 Amp my picture, dude, with mountains, moguls, trees and some awesome color!

Word Find

```
K  P  R  O  N  G  H  O  R  N  N  U
F  I  H  R  B  E  A  R  N  G  P  O
S  P  E  A  Y  Q  V  E  S  K  I  R
H  G  O  L  D  G  A  F  M  C  B  O
A  S  T  U  M  B  L  E  W  E  E  D
R  A  N  C  H  I  A  L  Z  J  A  E
I  U  V  M  O  U  N  T  A  I  N  O
E  B  E  K  R  H  C  A  B  I  N  H
N  C  F  W  S  J  H  Y  A  D  D  L
R  G  O  M  E  D  E  N  V  E  R  J
I  S  G  D  S  K  Q  X  T  E  S  I
D  T  U  N  N  E  L  K  B  R  C  M
```

AVALANCHE	DENVER	CABIN
RANCH	TUNNEL	TUMBLEWEED
BEAR	GOLD	MOUNTAIN
ELK	RODEO	HORSES
DEER	SKI	PRONGHORN

Bonus: Find small words not listed above and circle them in another color.

10

Cheeseburger

Louis Ballast once owned the Humpty Dumpty Drive-In in Denver. He wanted to jazz up his burgers and first tried adding peanut butter and then chocolate. Then, in 1935, he tried a slice of cheese and the cheeseburger was born. Luckily, cheeseburgers are popular everywhere since his drive-in is no longer around.

 What is your favorite topping on a cheeseburger?

Denver

Denver is the capital of Colorado and the largest city in Colorado. Denver is nicknamed "The Mile-High City," because it is exactly one mile above sea level. Denver was named by General William Larimer, after the governor of the Kansas Territory, Governor James W. Denver.

Draw a sun in the sky. On average, Denver has more sunny days than San Diego, California, each year.

The Zoo

Denver, Pueblo and Colorado Springs all have zoos. These zoos are home to animals that live in Colorado, like the bighorn sheep, as well as animals that are found in other countries, like lions and giraffes. Learn about these animals and their habitats at zoos and nature centers throughout the state.

 Black bears live in the Rocky Mountains and sometimes grizzly bears are seen there, too.

Pikes Peak

Over half a million people ride or climb to the very top of Pikes Peak each year. The very top of a mountain is called a summit or a peak. The summit of Pikes Peak is 14,110 feet above sea level. Pikes Peak is the most visited summit in the world. To reach the top, you can also take a special cog train.

 Circle the things you need to pack in your backpack or wear to climb to the top of Pikes Peak.

Buffalo Bill

Buffalo Bill was a soldier in the Civil War, a bison hunter, and a great horse-man. He is most famous for his Wild West Shows that featured western characters such as Annie Oakley, a legendary sharpshooter. Buffalo Bill's real name was William Frederick Cody.

At age 14, Bill Cody became a rider for the Pony Express, carrying mail by horseback across the west.

Mining

Colorado has many natural resources underground, including gold, silver, diamonds, coal and marble. People find these metals and minerals through digging or mining. The Tomb of the Unknown Soldier in Washington, D.C., was made out of marble from a Colorado quarry. The Colorado School of Mines is in Golden, Colorado.

Miners who "rushed" to Colorado for the gold rush were called Fifty-Niners, since many arrived in 1859.

Strike It Rich!

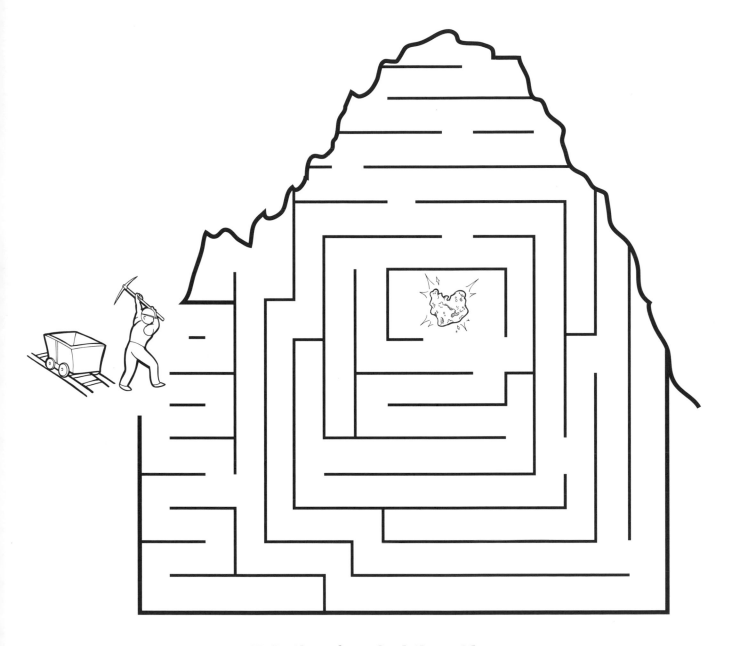

Help the miner find the gold.

 What rock or mineral would you most like to find in a mine?

Colorado Blue Columbine

The beautiful Colorado blue columbine is Colorado's state flower and often covers large meadows in spring. Hummingbirds and hawkmoths reach the sweet nectar in the flower's long spurs. Careful, don't pick them. It's illegal. They are protected by Colorado state law.

My flowers are pale blue to white. My leaves are green. Remember, if you find me, DON'T PICK ME!

American Pika

The pika is a small, hamster-like animal. It is also called a rock rabbit. It lives in the mountains and gathers grasses and flowers to eat. You might see small piles of grass, or "haystacks," it has set out to dry which it takes into its den for winter food. The pika has brown fur and a tail that is so short you can't see it.

Pikas are born blind and helpless, but grow fast. After 3 months, they gather their own flowers and grasses.

Wheat Farming

Driving across the plains of Colorado, you might see large tractors harvesting wheat. As Colorado's major food crop, wheat is sometimes called "prairie gold." Many breads, cookies and crackers are made from wheat.

 In 2007, Colorado ranked 8th for wheat producing states, valued at over $575 million!

Colorado Trees

Colorado has many beautiful trees. The native Colorado blue spruce, pictured here, is the state tree and is a popular Christmas tree. Colorado is also home to the largest forest of aspen trees in the country. Juniper trees grow in Colorado and can live up to 300 years.

The Colorado blue spruce can grow as tall as 156 feet, which is about as tall as a ten-story building!

Garden of the Gods

The popular Garden of the Gods is a unique park located in Colorado Springs. The park is famous for its giant red pinnacles. These rock formations were created by erosion, a process where wind and rain slowly wear away the stone over time. Only registered climbers with proper equipment are allowed to climb the rock formations.

 Can you see the rocks that look like kissing camels in the picture?

Rodeo

Rodeos are popular events in Colorado. The sport began when ranchers entered contests to test their working skills, like roping and herding cattle. Today rodeos include events like riding bulls and broncos (wild horses), or things like racing a horse around a set of barrels.

Rodeo clowns are fun to watch but their real job is to protect the riders bucked off dangerous bulls.

Rocky Mountain Bighorn Sheep

The male bighorn sheep, called a ram, has horns that can weigh up to 30 pounds! Rams use their horns to fight, sometimes charging each other at speeds of 20 miles per hour. The females, called ewes, also have horns. Bighorn sheep have split hooves for climbing, just like mountain goats.

 My baby lambs are born high on cliffs where others can't hurt them.

Judd Falls

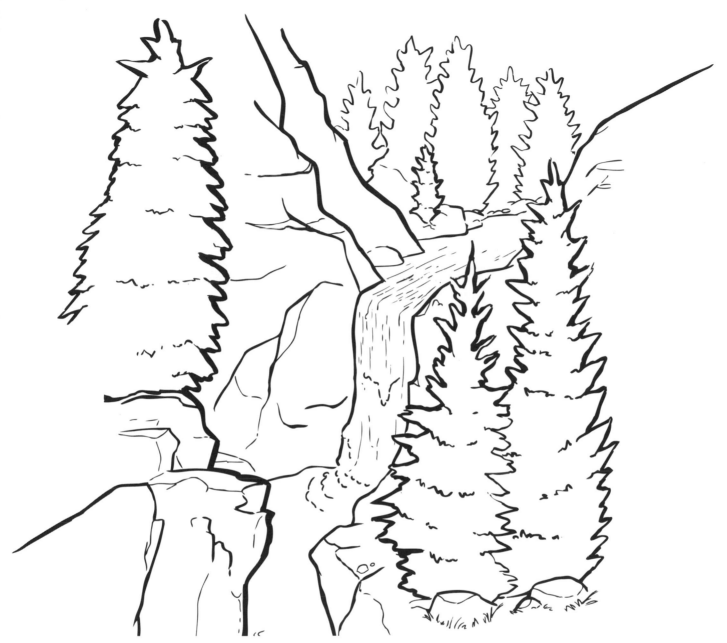

There are many waterfalls in Colorado, such as Seven Falls in Colorado Springs, Box Canyon Falls in Ouray, and Boulder Falls in Boulder Canyon. Ice and snow melt in the mountains and flow into the valleys. A cascade, such as Judd Falls near Gothic, is a waterfall that drops more than once.

Be careful near steep drop offs, especially if they are wet. The ground can by very slippery and dangerous.

Longhorn

A longhorn is a kind of cattle known for its long horns. The horns can be 4–6 feet long. They can live where no other cattle can survive. Longhorns can eat weeds, cactus and brush and can live many days without water.

 Longhorns are white, black, red or brown. They can be spotted or all one color. What color will you make me?

U.S. Air Force Academy

The U.S. Air Force Academy is located in Colorado Springs. Men and women go there to get an education and become officers in the U.S. Air Force. The U.S. Air Force was formed on September 18, 1949.

Color me: My jet is silver-gray. My jumpsuit is olive-green and my helmet is gray.

Yampa River

The Yampa River is the only major river in Colorado that isn't blocked by a dam. Many people enjoy rafting on the river. The best time to take a rafting trip is in spring when melted snow and ice fill the river with water. At other times the river can be too shallow for boating.

 Color the rocks reddish brown. Color the raft a bright color so it's easy to see.

Chief Black Kettle

Black Kettle was a chief of a Cheyenne Indian tribe. He was well known for trying to help settlers and the native Cheyenne people live together peacefully. He was respected by Indians and settlers alike.

 Colorado has been home to many other Native American peoples, such as the Arapaho, Navajo and Ute tribes.

Vinegar Hill

In the small town of Ouray, there is a hill that has been used for sledding for over 100 years. It is called Vinegar Hill and children enjoy sliding down the hill in the winter.

 Do you like to ice skate or snow ski? Ouray also has a skating rink and a ski hill for kids.

Olympic Training

The U.S. Olympic Team trains in Colorado Springs, Colorado. It is the headquarters for the U.S. Olympic Committee. You can visit the center and see the Olympic flame display and the U.S. Olympic Hall of Fame.

Color my letters red and my rings, from left to right, blue, yellow, black, green, red.

Wind Farms

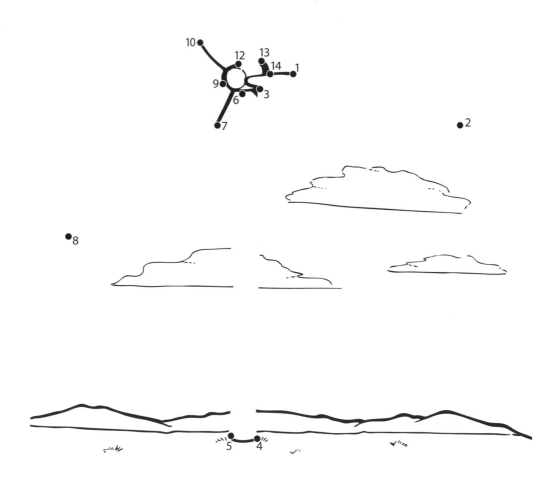

Connect the dots to see a machine that uses the wind to make electricity. Colorado's plains are almost always windy. Windmills make electricity for thousands of homes in Colorado. Wind farms, which are groups of windmills, provide clean, renewable energy.

 Wind farms help generate electricity. Name as many things in your house as you can that use electricity.

Eisenhower-Johnson Memorial Tunnel

Tunnels help people travel safely through the mountains, and Colorado has several of them. The Eisenhower-Johnson Memorial Tunnel is one of the most famous and is located about 60 miles west of Denver. At an elevation of 11,158 feet, it is the highest vehicle tunnel in the world. It is 1.6 miles long.

Over 10 million vehicles go through the Eisenhower-Johnson Memorial tunnel every year.

Lark Bunting

The lark bunting is a sparrow that lives on the great plains and eats insects and seeds on the ground. It nests on the ground, too. Most of the year it is brown, like other sparrows. But in spring, the male turns mostly black with white wing patches.

 The lark bunting is the state bird of Colorado.

What Does Not Belong in Colorado?

You can find many things in Colorado, but some things just don't belong.
Cross out everything you wouldn't find in Colorado.

Land Forms

Colorado has many interesting land forms, including mountains, prairies, grasslands, mesas and even sand dunes! The Great Sand Dunes are the tallest in the world at 750 feet tall. Visit Pawnee National Grasslands to see birds, mammals and wildflowers. Or check out Grand Mesa, the largest mesa in the world at over 40 miles long.

 A mesa has a flat top and steep cliffs, but Grand Mesa also has 300 lakes.

Dinosaurs

Many years ago, dinosaurs lived in what now is Colorado. Dinosaur Ridge, in Morrison, Colorado, is one of the world's most famous dinosaur fossil finds. Go to the visitor center to see dinosaur bones, tracks and fossils. The first stegosaurus bones were found at Dinosaur Ridge.

 Stegosaurus means "roof lizard" because of the plates on the "roof" of his back and spiked tail.

Native Americans

Many native peoples have called Colorado home. The Pueblos were farmers growing cotton and corn. The Cheyenne, Arapaho, Comanche and Pawneee were buffalo hunters. The Utes lived in the mountains and western plains and hunted elk, deer and bear.

 The Navajos are the largest native tribe in the U.S. They live around the Four Corners area of Colorado.

Yucca

Yucca plants grow on dry plains, prairies, and in rocky areas. The Navajo Indians used the root to make soap and the leaves to make sandals and mats. The yucca is important for the yucca moth, which only eats yucca. The moth helps the yucca plant too, as it can't make seeds without it.

My flowers are creamy white and my leaves are green and have a sharp needle on the end.

Adventure Sports

Colorado, with all its mountains, is the perfect place for extreme sports. In winter, snowboarding and ice climbing are popular. During the rest of the year, many people enjoy mountain biking, hang gliding, whitewater rafting, kayaking, riverboarding and other exciting sports.

 Color our lifejackets bright orange for safety.

Fill in the Blanks

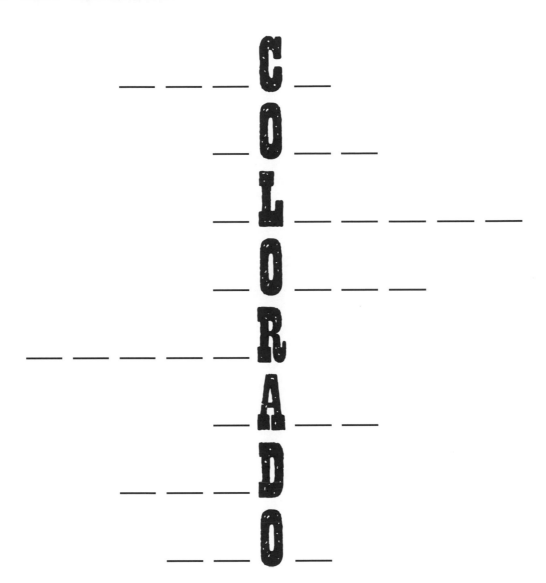

1. Where do cowboys live and work? (page 50)

2. What did miners rush to find in Colorado? (page 42)

3. Colorado Springs is home to what US training center? (page 31)

4. What is a favorite sport of cowgirls and cowboys? (page 23)

5. What is the capital of Colorado? (page 12)

6. Where is one of the favorite places to ski in Colorado? (page 9)

7. What alternate energy source blows across the Great Plains? (page 32)

8. What makes Colorado a fun place to play in winter? (page 9)

The Gold Rush

In 1859, gold was found in Colorado in Cherry Creek, near Denver City. Soon, many people came to Colorado to look for gold. When this happens, it is called a gold rush. The Colorado Gold Rush was the largest in American history. People looking for gold are called "prospectors."

 Draw and color nuggets of gold in the pan or in the river.

Ghost Towns

During the Gold Rush, many towns were created. But when the rush ended, the people suddenly left. When everyone leaves, it is called a ghost town. Quartz was a busy town for cargo going over the Cumberland Pass to Tincup. Now only a sign remains. Colorado has about 50 ghost towns.

Towns that grow very quickly due to the discovery of gold or other treasures are often called boomtowns.

Colorado Bingo

If you see one of the people, places, animals or objects on the Bingo card, mark it with an X. Be sure to mark the free space in the middle. If you get five Xs in a row, you win! Don't forget to yell "Bingo!"

B	I	N	G	O
COWBOY	YUCCA	MOUNTAIN	BIGHORN SHEEP	COMBINE
GHOST TOWN	CHEESEBURGER	TUNNEL	HORSE	OLYMPIC RINGS
COLORADO BLUE COLUMBINE	FISHING	FREE	SKIER	DENVER
ELK	QUEEN'S CROWN	SAND DUNES	TRAIN	LONGHORN
MESA	ANTELOPE	LARK BUNTING	WINDMILL	COLORADO BLUE SPRUCE

 Jim Swigert, an astronaut on Apollo 13, was born in Denver. He received a Presidential Medal of Freedom.

Fishing

Many people come to Colorado to fish. Many kinds of fish live in Colorado, including trout, salmon, bass and walleye. Some fish live in the cold mountain lakes. Others live in the warmer prairie lakes or in streams or rivers.

The largest rainbow trout caught in Colorado weighed 19 pounds, 10 ounces and was 34 inches long.

Four Corners

The Four Corners is a region in the U.S. where four states touch each other. The four states are Colorado, Arizona, New Mexico and Utah. There is a monument at the site where you can stand in all four states at the same time.

 The Four Corners area is also home to two Native American tribes, the Navajo and Ute Nations.

Kit Carson

Christopher Houston "Kit" Carson was a trapper, a guide and a soldier who explored the Colorado region and beyond. He guided many people to the western frontier. He became a legend in his own time and he was featured in novels, poems and songs.

My height was only 5'6" and yet people told lots of tall tales about me.

Get Me Home!

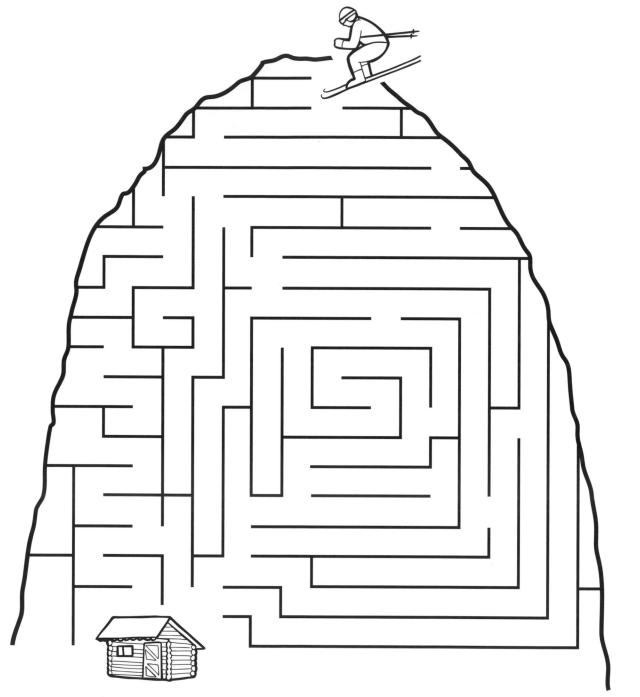

Help the skier find his way down the mountain and back to his cabin.

Many skiers come to Colorado for its high peaks and fresh blankets of snow.

Elk are a kind of deer. In fact, they are one of the largest types of deer in the world. Only moose are bigger. Male elk are called bulls. They grow antlers and call loudly to attract female elk, which are called cows. In the early 1900s, there were less than 2,000 elk left in Colorado. Today, they are at least 250,000.

 I lose my antlers every year at the end of winter. It takes only 3–4 months to grow them to full size.

What's My Job?

Connect the dots to see someone who works on a ranch. He takes care of animals by feeding them and giving them water. He does lots of other work on the ranch, such as fixing fences and daily chores. And he competes in rodeos too!

I am a _____. Draw the tools I use or animals you think I might work with.

Yellow-Bellied Marmot

Yellow-bellied marmots live on mountains, usually above 6,500 feet. They live in open rocky areas, where they make burrows under rocks. They hide there if they see an animal that might eat them, such as a coyote, a fox or an eagle. If they sense danger, they whistle warnings to other marmots.

I mostly like to eat the leaves and flowers of many plants. Color my side fur yellow.

Queen's Crown

Queen's crown grows in the wet areas along streams in the high country of Colorado. Since soil is often poor where this wildflower grows, it stores sap in its leaves the way desert plants do. Native Americans ate the leaves raw or boiled. Its scientific name means "rose root," because its roots smell like roses.

 I have pink flowers in summer and my leaves turn flaming red in the fall.

Red Rocks Park

Denver's Red Rocks Park is known for its huge, red rocks that were once part of a mountain range. Over millions of years, wind and water wore away the rock, producing what we see today. The park is also home to an amphitheatre (a theater with outdoor seating) that has been built into the rocks.

The amphitheatre at Red Rocks has enough seating for 9,450 people. Many famous people perform here.

Word Find

```
C O L L E D F G M B B J
P B I G H O R N I E G P
H E V A U R A D N C A C
V J A L K I R N E K H O
A D I N O S A U R Y T L
S I L V E R P W U T E O
O B G E N E A P I K E R
S T E V E N H A T M P A
T M B D S N O W C H E D
E V I N D I A N S J E O
O L J U N I P E R L R Y
W C O W B O Y E L P A Q
```

SILVER	PIKE	PAWNEE
COWBOY	VAIL	JUNIPER
INDIANS	UTE	DINOSAUR
COLORADO	MINER	BIGHORN
SNOW	TEEPEE	ARAPAHO

Katharine Lee Bates

In 1893, Katharine Lee Bates, a poet and a professor of English at Wellesley College, took a train trip to Colorado Springs. Inspired by the trip, she began to write a poem at the top of Pikes Peak. The poem became the song "America The Beautiful."

In the song, the phrase "from sea to shining sea" refers to the Pacific Ocean and Atlantic Ocean.

Horses

Horses have played an important role in Colorado. Horses were used to explore the mountains and backcountry. They also worked on ranches, pulling heavy wagons and moving herds of cattle. Horses are still important today, working on ranches and appearing in rodeos.

 State park rangers use horses as an efficient way to get around on rough terrain.

Royal Gorge Bridge

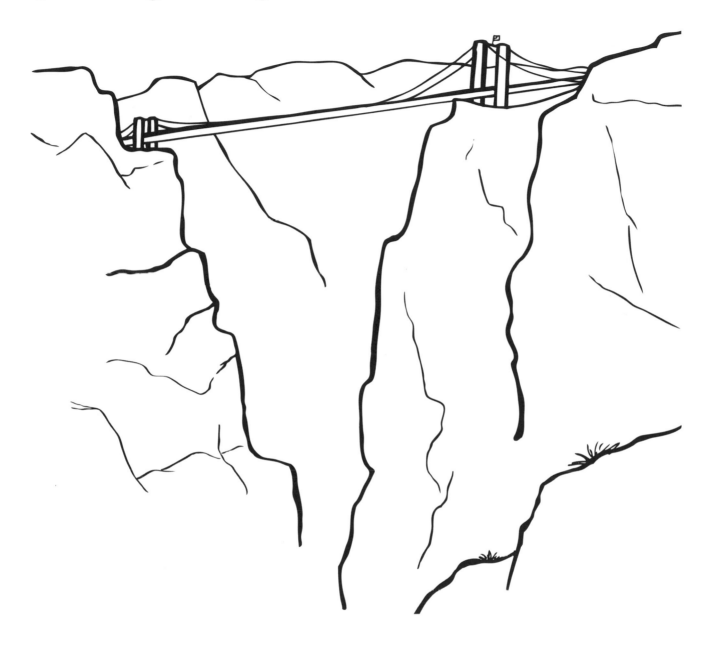

The Royal Gorge is a canyon on Colorado's Arkansas River, near Cañon City. It is the site of the Royal Gorge Bridge, the highest suspension bridge in the world. The bridge is 1,053 feet above the river and is 1,260 feet long. No fishing from the bridge!

 The bridge's walkway has 1,292 wooden planks.

Pronghorn

Pronghorns are the fastest mammals in the Americas. They are almost as fast as the cheetah, the fastest land animal in the world. Pronghorns live in large herds on grasslands and eat many plants that livestock cannot eat. Although commonly called antelopes, pronghorns are not related to those African animals.

 I can leap with all four feet in the air at once. This is called a pronk or stot. Which word do you like?

Quiz Your Parents

1. What is the meaning of the word Colorado?

2. What is the largest flat top mountain in Colorado?

3. What are the three landforms in Colorado?

4. Which animal in Colorado pronks or stots?

5. What do Coloradoans refer to as "prairie gold?"

6. What is the state bird of Colorado?

7. Name five Native American tribes that have called Colorado home.

8. What insect is important to the Yucca plant?

9. What are some extreme sports in Colorado?

10. Why were some gold miners called Fifty-Niners?

11. What states make up the Four Corners region?

12. What are female elk called?

13. Do bighorn sheep females have horns?

14. What river does the Royal Gorge Bridge cross?

15. Name four professional sports teams from Colorado.

16. Who wrote the poem "America The Beautiful" that later became a song?

(answers on page 62)

Leadville

Leadville is the highest incorporated city in the U.S. at 10,152 feet. It is one of the oldest silver-mining camps in the world. During World War II, the Army trained soldiers on the ski slopes around Leadville before they were sent to Europe.

Color me with dark greens, make Turquoise Lake in the background blue, and put snow on the mountains.

Name the Animals

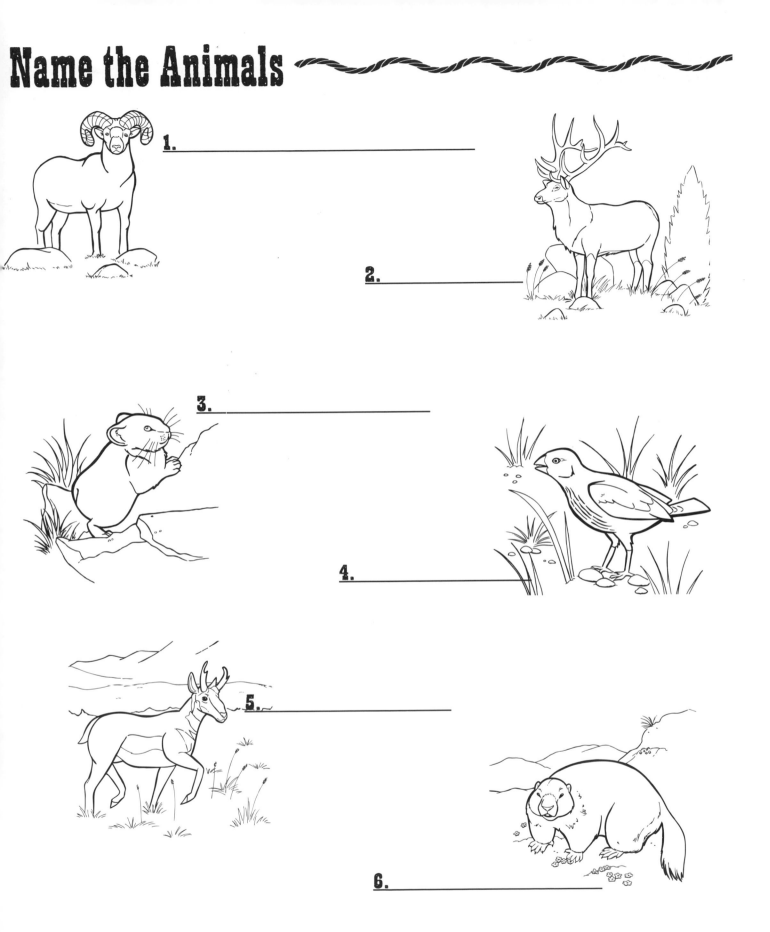

1. _____

2. _____

3. _____

4. _____

5. _____

6. _____

Bonus: What do you remember the most about each animal?

Answers

Page 3

rectangle

7

Utah, Wyoming, Nebraska, Kansas, Oklahoma, New Mexico, Arizona

Page 10—Word Find

```
K  P  R  O  N  G  H  O  R  N  N  U
F  I  H  R  B  E  A  R  N  G  P  O
S  P  E  A  Y  Q  V  E  S  K  I  R
H  G  O  L  D  G  A  F  M  C  B  O
A  S  T  U  M  B  L  E  W  E  E  D
R  A  N  C  H  I  A  L  Z  J  A  E
I  U  V  M  O  U  N  T  A  I  N  O
E  B  E  K  R  H  C  A  B  I  N  N
N  C  F  W  S  J  H  Y  A  D  D  L
R  G  O  M  E  D  E  N  V  E  R  J
I  S  G  D  S  K  Q  X  T  E  S  I
D  T  U  N  N  E  L  K  B  R  C  M
```

Page 14—Pikes Peak Backpack

gloves, hiking boots, hat, toilet paper, compass, water, map

Page 17—Miner Maze

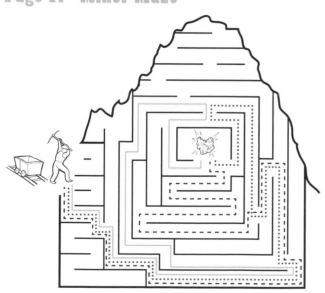

Page 35—What Does Not Belong in Colorado

Page 41—Fill in the Blanks

1. ranch
2. gold
3. Olympic
4. rodeo
5. Denver
6. Vail
7. wind
8. snow

Answers

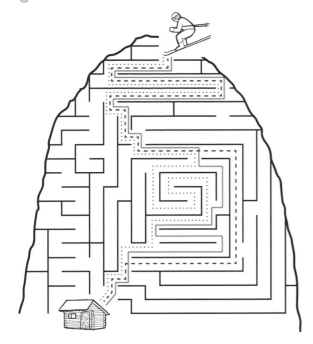

cowboy

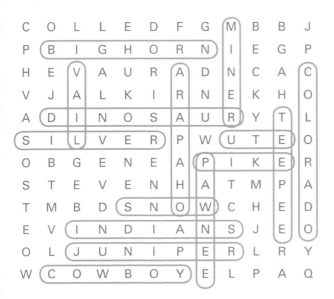

1. red colored
2. Grand Mesa
3. mountains, prairie grassland, mesa, sand dunes
4. pronghorn
5. wheat
6. lark bunting
7. Arapaho, Cheyenne, Pueblos, Comanche, Ute, Apache, Navajo, Comanche, Pawnee
8. yucca moth
9. snowboarding, ice climbing, mountain biking, hang gliding, whitewater rafting, kayaking, river boarding
10. Because they came to Colorado for the gold rush in 1859.
11. Colorado, Arizona, New Mexico, Utah
12. cows
13. yes
14. Arkansas River
15. Colorado Avalanche (hockey)
    Colorado Mammoth (lacrosse)
    Colorado Rapids (soccer)
    Colorado Rockies (baseball)
    Denver Broncos (football)
    Denver Nuggets (basketball)
16. Katharine Lee Bates

Answers

About the Author

Paula Ellis grew up in a small town in central Michigan. Her love of the outdoors and travel began at a young age. She is the mother of two children, daughter Heather, and son Todd David. Through travel and everyday experiences, she taught them to appreciate, respect and enjoy all of creation.

Paula enjoys being a grandma, exploring the wilderness, traveling and watching her four grandchildren grow and learn about the world in which they live.

She believes children are eager to learn about their environment, whether they're playing in the backyard, traveling across the country or catching bugs on a camping trip. To that end, she strives to encourage children of all ages to see and explore all the fascinating things around them.

Every now and then you will find her standing in the lake at sunset, fishing.

About the Illustrator

Anna Kaiser is an illustrator who loves making art for children. She enjoys exploring different mediums and subject matter in her work, though creating animal characters are her absolute favorite. Anna likes the challenge of working with different materials but is most familiar with clay, various three-dimensional media and acrylic paints.

When she isn't creating art, Anna enjoys long bike rides, always taking her camera along to photograph the journey. She has a fascination for birds and can often be found with her eyes peeled to the sky hoping to catch a glimpse of her feathered friends.

Anna currently resides in her home state of Wisconsin with her three marvelous goldfish, Spike, Julia and Goliath. She would like to give a special thanks to Erik Christenson for his everlasting love, understanding and support on this project. If you would like to see more of Anna's illustrations, visit her website at www.annakaiser.net.